Dance

Acro Dance

By Trudy Becker

level 2 little blue readers

www.littlebluehousebooks.com

Little Blue House is distributed by North Star Editions:
sales@northstareditions.com | 888-417-0195

Produced for Little Blue House by Red Line Editorial.

Photographs ©: Shutterstock Images, cover, 4, 7, 9, 19, 24 (top right); iStockphoto, 10, 13, 15, 16, 21, 22–23, 24 (top left), 24 (bottom left), 24 (bottom right)

Library of Congress Control Number: 2022919418

ISBN
978-1-64619-826-9 (hardcover)
978-1-64619-855-9 (paperback)
978-1-64619-910-5 (ebook pdf)
978-1-64619-884-9 (hosted ebook)

Printed in the United States of America
Mankato, MN
082023

About the Author

Trudy Becker lives in Minneapolis, Minnesota. She likes exploring new places and loves anything involving books.

Table of Contents

Twist and Turn

A boy moves across the floor.

He turns and flips.

He does a trick.

A girl jumps and twirls. Then she bends her legs back.

Another girl dances.
Her moves are strong
and smooth.
She is doing acro dance.

What Is Acro Dance?

Acro dance is a kind of dance.

Dancers do tricks with their bodies.

They jump and flip.

They need good balance.

Balance helps them
stay up.

Acro dancers use
their muscles.
They also use teamwork
to dance together.

muscles

teacher

Learning How

Acro dancers practice.

They learn the tricks.

Teachers help them

stay safe.

Dancers wear tight outfits.

The clothes stay close to their bodies.

That helps them move.

Acro dancers stretch before dancing. Then they can bend far and turn smoothly.

Before a show, dancers
get ready.
They take deep breaths.
It is time to acro dance!

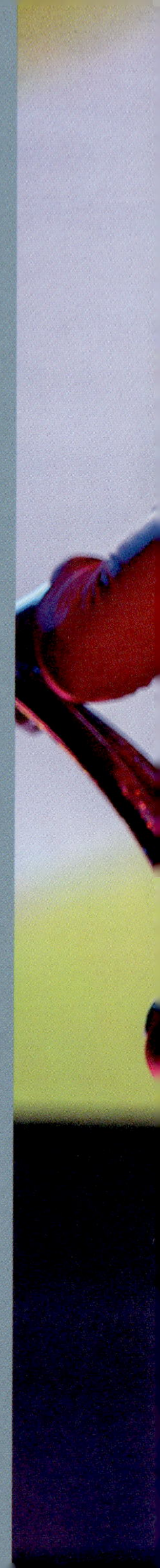

Glossary

bend

outfit

muscles

stretch

Index